Works and Days

Bernadette Mayer

Works and Days

A NEW DIRECTIONS BOOK

Manufactured in the United States of America
New Directions Books are printed on acid-free paper
First published as New Directions Paperbook 1341 in 2016

Library of Congress Cataloging in Publication Data
Names: Mayer, Bernadette, author.
Title: Works and days / Bernadette Mayer.
Description: New York : New Directions Publishing, [2016]
Identifiers: LCCN 2016007202 | ISBN 9780811225175 (softcover : acid-free paper)
Classification: LCC PS3563.A952 A6 2016 | DDC 811/.54—dc23
LC record available at http://lccn.loc.gov/2016007202

10 9 8 7 6 5 4 3

New Directions Books are published for James Laughlin
by New Directions Publishing Corporation
80 Eighth Avenue, New York 10011

Spring Journal

March 20 to June 21

Author's note

Thanks to Hesiod for providing the title, *Works and Days*, and to my sister Rosemary for pointing it out to me. "Soule Sermon" was written for Futurefarmers and performed at their show at the Guggenheim Museum. "Geology Night Sky" was written as an introduction to Richard Grossinger's book *The Night Sky*. The text is interspersed with seemingly random agglomerations of letters from a daily word game, the jumble. The book ends with writings that include all the letters of the alphabet. Thank you to Alan Casline for publishing some of these poems in *All Fall Down*, Benevolent Bird Press. Thanks to my helpers, Philip Good and Marie Warsh.

April 15

Payment for some Mohican land:
     300 guilders in sewan
     8 blankets
     25 ells of duffel
     4 fathoms of strouding
     20 shirts
     6 guns
     50 lbs of powder
     50 bars of lead
     4 caps
     10 kettles
     10 axes
     10 adzes
     2 lbs of vermillion
     20 scissors
     20 looking glasses
     100 fish hooks
     100 awls
     100 nails
     4 rolls of tobacco
     100 pipes
     100 bottles of rum
     1 barrel of beer
     200 knives
     10 coats
     14 kettles

Walking Like a Robin

take 3 or 4 steps then stop
look smell taste touch & hear
is there anything to eat?
oh look, there's some caviar
it must be my birthday, thanks
i must be very old, like seventy
i guess i'm falling apart, i'll just
sew myself back together but will it last?
please take a piece of me back home, each piece
is anti-war and don't pay your rent, in fact
remember: property is robbery, give everybody
everything, other birds walk this way too

Soule Sermon

It could be that I am a fish or was one once

I remember thinking Aristotle was an asshole

It is like a dark, crazy garden

I didn't know then about shoes & shoelessness

Cultivated away from light & bathed

How vital & symbolic it was to the cynics

In a profligate torrent of sulphur

This was in the days when philosophy

& clams which live there grow to an enormous size

It was your main avocation, your vacation your way

Like pampered dahlias

Of paying your mortgage

Rocks found in the Achaean crust

Thought Socrates, philosophers

2,500 million years ago or more

Should converse with shoemakers

The atmosphere lacked oxygen

Whereas Aristotle felt they should talk with kings

The oxygen slowly built up over a billion years

We in the 21st century still have this dichotomy

In one of the obscure parts of the palaeontological consciousness

Remember in the 20th century when we

With other jelly-fish-like curiosities

Tried to convince our elders

Ocean-going medusae

That hippiedom was the answer

This was when the seas advanced over continents

They'd always say what would you replace the system with

A rich sedimentary record

We'd say everything should be free

There are four kinds of jokes:

Remember sitting at that table

The mother-in-law joke, the sexual innuendo

It was hard to swallow the mashed potatoes

Jokes about foreigners, jokes about politicians

But we were right all along

Charles Doolittle Walcott discovered the burgess shale

Aristotle did us all a great disservice

On the surface of carboniferous flakes

By famously advocating cause & effect

Fossil leaves carry the fine veins we know

We'd all have been better off going sideways or backwards

Like or from living leaves

Things don't lead upward & get improved

If it seems soulless to attribute

Nor is everything higher better

The glories of arboreal form

North isn't up; south isn't down

To natural design alone

My dog Hector never wore shoes

Underestimating an appropriate sense of wonder

Socrates, a cynic, used to hang out

At the extraordinary & creative inventiveness

At the shop of Simon the shoemaker

Which life has repeatedly shown

Where he found thought more relevant

I became a land-dwelling mammal in a house

Than that of sandaled kings

100 years old with a stone foundation

Idiotic uptown types of thinking

It used to be a Christian church

Spawned by the values of paintings

You can see the rafters upstairs

& odd rare fruit, the nuts nobody's heard of

A rabbi made it a boarding house

Let me tell you how Hector got his name:

You need waterproof shoes to be here

Our friend Russell, descendant of a family of Days

Because we are near two creeks

Was sitting in Inwood Park reading the Iliad

The Kinderhook & the Tsatsawassa

When a woman approached him with Hector

Sometimes they overflow onto the ground you walk on

She said, "I have to go to Troy, do you want this dog?"

It's halfway between the sunniest & least sunny places

Like Hector, I wear the same things outside as in

Halfway between Albany & Pittsfield, Mass.

Of the Palaeozoic eras there are: Cambrian

I'd like to be free as the birds of the air, wouldn't thee?

Ordovician, Silurian, Devonian

Hector the dog bought the farm but never wore shoes

Permian & carboniferous, Jurassic comes later

Did you ever hear that politicians

& psychopaths use the same mental stuff

In different ways? Did you know that many of the fossils

Found at the burgess shale were misclassified at first

To accommodate the discoverer's view of life? Have you

Ever heard of the burgess shale? did you ever

Have a trilobite? When Steven Jay Gould was growing up

The other kids called him Fossil Face. I have worked

Hard all my life & I still have no house, no wife

No car, no flat-screen t.v. what does life mean?

The answer is somewhere in hallucigenia

A weird & unfollowed offspring

Of some evolutionary stem of life

Found in the burgess shale in British Columbia

Nobody'll ever know where it would've led

You can find its picture on the internet

Which is now the memory of everybody

Wouldn't it be nice for gas station attendants

To give you gas for free? Even better

Cars don't need gas & they are left

By the side of the road for you if you need one

Right now, the founder of Facebook

Is on the cover of *Time* magazine, why not you

Or me or Sir Thomas Browne or that guy who'll frown

When presented with potatoes that are mashed

Not smashed or a martini made wrongly?

I have more shoes than you do, look

They're all here but mine won't fit you

My feet are large for a tiny woman

But small for an award-winning restauranteur

Selling food from Brooklyn in Manhattan

& finding wine on the sea floor

That's been there longer than a fossil

Could it be true? Philosophy chics

Kiss better than paleontology chics

Do tell! The very best kissers are women who

Hang out at the sidebar drinking aquavit straight

Till the cows come home, I dare to opine

Be a carpenter! Tie the curtain with

A smaller curtain, it might grow

To be a full curtain or

Don't tie it, whaddo I care?

Getting down to brass tacks on an ocean

Of dinosaurs in haystacks: almost never

Does a peninsula get surrounded

Like in an old famous western, by water

Hey ho nobody's home

No meat, no drink, no money

Have I none, put your hands together

For the shoemaker's quantum peninsula

At ultima thule near uluru!

Do words actually have a meaning?

What does actually actually mean?

Can I possess a vision like an object, like

Shoes. These are my shoes, but are these my lack of

Shoes?

That is, is my shoelessness mine?

Does I am barefoot mean I am shoeless?

Is my soul also shoeless?

What does it mean for a soul to have no shoes?

Does it mean my soul lacks support?

I saw a sale on innersoles at a shoe store recently.

Maybe an inner sole is what my soul needs. We

Should ask the man on the street.

He says, I've got soul. Might he mean the

Other kind of soul?

Is there any solution to this conundrum?

Isn't a solution an Aristotelian concept?

If we prefer Socrates, do we then not believe in

Solutions? All of western culture?

Did Aristotle do irreparable damage to us souls?

All of western culture?

I always thought of a soul as a giant communion

Wafer in the middle of your body. Is the soul the heart?

When I go to sleep, is that sleep my sleep

Or everybody's who's asleep at the time?

As if sleep were a world, always there, you entered into,

Like the dream world. Was that my dream then?

Scram, get outta my face! Did the mail come?

Will you get the mail?

Is having shoes red & not having shoes green?

Alec Baldwin looks a lot like Alec Baldwin

April 14 a Monday

Let's begin again. It's unnaturally warm, the
hornet's gone.

April 15

Today's the day of the wintry mix, preceded by thunder and wind.
Whether this will happen I don't know; it's what I've been told. Poor
Phil is stuck on the thruway, returning from Passover. Perhaps, some
accident creating a delay. I don't like the way they say, "that acci-
dent has been cleaned up, cleared away." As if the cars should not be
stopped. They're dinner dishes.

April 16

Snow, no thunder, where am I?

April 17

The tomentose part of the hepatica is up, that's all.
No bloodroots. Are cars as unstoppable as spring? The sun
shines bright around me facing south, it's 34 degrees.
Not a creature is stirring, not even a mouse. Birds stir.

After moving here, I wrote this poem. Everybody said it didn't
say the right things and I sent it to the wrong person.
You can still see snow on the hill on the other side of the
Kinderhook creek.

The Great Outdoors

I left NYC because it took
So long to get out the door
In the city the streets are
Your hallways, I am a mole person
I wanted to transcend growing up in Brooklyn
Now out the door I can see
A creek monster or rainbow
In the woods, I can build things
Without anybody seeing me. I can make piles
Of autumn leaves, wood, yarn, snow
And cover them with a tarp

April 18

Now it starts, Good Friday. Today's the day you can plant beans and peas. If you're a practicing Catholic you keep silent from noon to 3 p.m. in honor of the suffering of Christ on the cross. When my mother was dying of breast cancer, a priest came by to tell her that the pain she was experiencing was equivalent to Christ's on the cross. But Jesus Christ had no breasts. 36 degrees.

There's a lot of sadomasochism inherent in the Catholic Church, witness St. Sebastian or the cannibalism of transubstantiation.

To learn more read the lives of the saints and martyrs. One sewed herself together because all her body parts were falling off. In New Orleans, today you go around to bars on Good Friday, to find five you can see a church from the door of.

Thin Places

Thwick-thwack paddywack
Give that dog a bone
This old man is going home

But there's nothing there
I've had it with these clouds
I'm going to the lower world
Through a thin place
Like a chipmunk's hole
If a leaning tree falls down
The other three parts will fall too
An anarchist believes governments don't work
How could they? All those pipes
And wires under the ground
Not to mention the roots that were there first
One is the poison-ivy root system
Where garter snakes are known to hatch
Where our bench used to be
Until it was thrown into the creek
By assholes, where a tree fell
Next to a pile of no man's lands, by the way
You shouldn't have to pay for heat, rich people
Duped everyone into thinking everything isn't free
So let's start over now, philosophically too
And dig deep geothermal holes forgetting war
And the news on t.v. and make our livings
Doing nothing but local root-mapping
And giving everyone five, hundred, thousands, billions, trillions

April 19

Last year a man came by telling us there was a disabled copperhead crossing the road. Copper makes me think of hallucinations. I read a book once about a small town in France where everybody ate the local bread on which ergot had grown on the flour. One man hallucinated his head was made of copper. Another counted the same 6 window panes over and over. Copper is a conductor of electricity. It's 55 degrees. It was sunny, now not. Tomorrow, Easter Sunday is 4/20 – pot day, so be sure to smoke marijuana at 4:20 on 4/20. If you can't you'll have to do April Fool's Day again dressed as a red-winged blackbird pretending to be a grackle.

April 20

Dream: "her father was a raisin." Jay the farmer next to Bill, stopped by to ask if it would be ok to drop off 2 cords of wood. I went to the creek and saw one fisherman and one bird.

seora   mpost   preetx   starig   trecp   suymh

hmyus   tidfet   cucusa   slatb   cleri   wrinye

Ice Bucket

At the exact moment I went
To the mailbox to get some delicious
Andy the mailman drove up and said
    "let's trade"

I Am a Coyote

On the go
I'll fool you
Into thinking
You're one too
Who's to say
I can't do it?

Jay may have lost two fingertips in the wood-splitter, told to us as if it happened every day. Oddly I'm reading *Russ and Daughters* in which an aging schmoozer tells of one of the daughters slicing off two fingertips in the slicer and having them sewn back on by a doctor who's a customer.

The First Wasp of Spring

There's a wasp in here
I'm keeping my eye on it
It fell behind my desk
It seems rejuvenated
It doesn't talk
Like a zoo animal
It crawls back and forth
Then falls and crawls
On the back of my desk
A weary wasp
Climbing now to the top of the pane
Investigating the hook
Then down oh up again
Then gone oh perched
Oh fallen down
Mid-pane it stops, is gone
Next morning it's back
Or I'm back, it's still here
On the sunnier pane
It's almost Passover
More full of life
Loving the crack in the pane
It's on the picture frame now

April 21

The Monday between Easter and Earth Day.
Phil's mulching the blueberry bush in the hopes the poison ivy won't
take over. Today last year Max drove a small U-Haul full of Rosemary's
work up here. It said Mom's Attic which is where it was going. We
couldn't get all the sculptures upstairs so the amphora's on top of the
refrigerator. On the way to Wassaic, driving Max to Metro-North we
passed through Webutunk and Amenia.

glefan pleeo fuyin stumco adfair riafda

slyte etyls ceenf sirnap panris stturyzirep

Leg of Lamb

A line
Break could reflect
The way the sun breaks
Through the clouds or breakfast
Or this rainbow begins here
And then's over
There too
The aurora borealis can be
All over the sky
Wherever you look
Not in one place
Like north
Up and down
East and west, southwest
Side-saddle, acrobatic as a squirrel
A parhelion (sun pillar) appears
On each side of the sun in cities
Is an e-mail directional?
I guess I'll just think
And be as smart as in dreams
So they won't come to get me
And take me away to
Zanzibar, the mental asylum. The hospital
The jail, turn the line'n you wind up in
Antarctica Australia Mesoamerica mesothelioma
The middle of nowhere somewhere
You've left all the slush
Behind back there where the line begins, ends
Do we notice, yes
Are we sorry? No, maybe, always
Sometimes never we will never come to an end because
Starting over's our addiction, a dead
End and where does that leave
Us?

April 22

In Missouri turtles are crossing the roads. There's buds on the lilac bush, many chives, the hepatica, some green leaves, a blue pickup. The guy who bought the field and turned it into a lawn, seems to be carrying a rifle, hope he doesn't shoot me. I heard shots, maybe just aimless, maybe the rifle was a stick. These grackles seem like prison guards.

periz ngaa bulmet eeendl ldneee zagel dirog

forpi agents lurty berel slipho gunole elonig

April 23

Gloom and rain. The heat turns on. A cardinal.
It's grayer than a doornail.

dusko nirbg gbrin warley yelraw simaco ocamis

tmaid diamt sayet teluto gemnat tanmeg aview

Dangerous Solamente Sense

Dangerous are eyes
The mountain laurel seeds
Have gotten into everything
Psychology is lucky
That it makes no sense to me
I still think angles and angels are the same
And no backyard is ever overrated
Superb without beginnings, middles
Or ends like a fortune not like
A preoccupation with time which
Involves movement, hilly upstart
With a gun, he fires it, that sound
It's a rifle, why? A duck flies away
Using circles, a certain amount of money
Say $11.16 becomes the cost of cremation
On main street or under an old el
You should go to the lobster support group

April 24

It's Arbor Day eve. Words chosen at random by cutting circles in a piece of paper placed over workshop's poems. Making syntax not sense, the illusion of sense. It's like going to the weight room. I think the bluebirds will occupy that house.

sliposwrapl   kimps   vleebcorrus   dulgesvhlys

fatsf   cucorn   tgent   tnegot   ydold   dlody   chumh

awayir   awryia

pcemker   pacemaker

peacemark cream cake   cracker crepe pan

saw a scarlet elf cap (mushroom) in the woods.
Also the leaves of the trillium.

Why Are There Thorns?

In perfect alignment, you
The paper, let my words wind up
Over to you, in your vicinity, it's like
Infinity like a lily pad like a defrocked priest
Or nun a deconsecrated church an excommunicated
Atheist fellow a whirling dervish shrink-wrapped
Books the immaculate conception that guy's
Not home he's missing from the tabernacle
He's lost I'm found it's a miracle to behold
Your erect penis the duck's corkscrew vagina
The forensics on a t.v. show the full-frontal nudity
Of a star the elegant dreaming universe, when
Did you get here? When will you take the train back?
Art for art's sake? I don't think so
Let's start over begin again now who could
Ever meet me there then? You think so
I doubt it yes it's your eighth thought out
Of an infinity of utopian giggles humming
In the background of the empire city which is
Nowhere you would ever go without my relatives
And all their belongings on top of a truck
When the mountains turn blue the beer is cold
Yes it's 8 it must be 8 it is number 8
A path where no man thought

The "Go Away" Welcome Mat of Steve Levine

Never saw dandelions in the field before
Marking like on a map where the rivers'd be
When the snow melts in the field, it looks
Like a map too: I can pass for a cognizant human
Mostly everywhere near are planes flying to scrunching
Locations, doesn't everybody know everything
When the internet provides us a common memory?
So what's different? The personal history
Of each, like as if when we began and ended
So did the world we see, these dandelions, this gloom
Aren't me exactly but my horror at not being
Loved, ending when his line ends, but it won't
Till I fall like a squirrel down the birdfeeder pole
To the seeds that for Sarah's mother start flowers
Sunflowers, maybe our seeds are genetically engineered.
Genetically engineering plants is like sterilization.
Let the plants reproduce! says my sign. I carry it
To all the demonstrations of the past, present and emu

Beware! A Grey Cloud!

I saw the great blue heron
Twice today
You know how you can
Startle a covey of quail?
There it was, waiting
Where the GBF* cleared a space near the promontory
Over where the two creeks meet
The heron ate my heart raw
And before I died I saw
Two goddesses: chance and change
Like whirling dervishes they turned
Like a roulette wheel they stopped
At East Nassau, 4/11/2012
"you will forget everything"
said change
"you will forget everything"
said chance
and rolling around in the mud
I thought:
Zebra tongues are black, willow

*the guy who bought the field

The Oyster Barn

I am the new blue angel
Nobody in Pensacola
Where crows glide like pelicans
Thought I'd ever come

I'm better than a Louisiana blackberry
Baked in a crumble like the sizzling gulf's froth
That boils in your toes till there's a heated
Debate about beneficacy
And what about the children?
Oh Rosa Parks I thought things'd
Be better than this

Yield to Opposing Traffic

Sometimes crosswinds are not the only danger
Watch for thunderstorms, fire, tornadoes and traffic
If it is opposing you should know what to do
Panic? No yield
Yielding can be a good thing
Large hail is coming
There's an owl in this room
I dreamt a cow put out a forest fire
By warning a bear about the weather
But what is the wooden indian's name?
The one in the old song
What is the zoo animal that starts with the letter K?
I'm trying to remember the name of the Italian guy from Astoria
It's not a kangaroo
Jack Hanna brought it on t.v. in New Mexico
Where roadrunners run across the road

Renaming Things

Flowers ... plants
Clover ... lovers
Thistle ... stick-in-the-mud
Goldenrod ... ne'er-do-well
Unidentifiable shrub ... isis' blood
Grass ... cheveux de spectre
Celandine ... cowering DNA
Woodland sunflower ... how strange
Field fern ... bronze idol
Bramble bush ... attacker of Bernadette
Poison ivy ... ménage à trois
Grass ... hector's lunch
Wild aster ... smart mouth pucker
Dandelion ... liminal lettuce
Yarrow ... the bobby mcgee
Thimble berry ... tom's tart
Bloodroot ... dragon buddies
Sycamore ... quark ladder
Dragonflies ... braidkissers
Butterfly ... indigo tourism

(with the members of the Rootdrinker workshop)

April 25

It's Arbor Day now. We should have a Rock Day, a Darning Needle Day, a Shell Day. Russell Day could be a day for eating artichokes, or there could be an Artichoke Day, it's Poetry Month. Today we went on a shopping expedition, planted a blue grass, and now Phil is transferring seeds that sprouted too soon to larger spaces. We forgot to buy potatoes and stamps but we remembered the leg of lamb and other more decadent things. We saw flowers, tempting azaleas and blooming dogwood sprigs. Before it's warm enough to grow plants here, the stores sell plants and flowers to inspire you, grown indoors or maybe to remind you that you can grow them indoors too. It's the season of temptation, about plants, incipience, coming just after the season of catalogue reading, of envisioning those tomatoes, don't touch!

faunit   rinuaf   lohwol   lowhol   veerfluvat   tinday

westwftreex   wardf   fdraw   cesbit   tibsec   lomans

April 26

I'm reading a book by Margaret Atwood called *Blind Assassin* because I was looking for the phrase "blonde assassin" from an Emily Dickinson poem in which it's a bee and I happened upon this book at the library. It's a *Downton Abbey*-type tale that takes place in Canada, Port Ticonderoga. The rich man is a manufacturer of buttons. Among the rich men I've met one made bobby pins, one shower-curtain holders, and one cassette-tape containers. Another Velcro.

snomal slebs socru deeibs sbieed mayrac caryem

todub budot clawr rwalc turopo urpot oporut

Enter If You Dare

Urban light
Conundrum columbum
Olly olly income free
Ghost duck not space duck
Enter vain tango, ha

Tango tango aqua zen
Allez beer, beer allez
Sects bifurcate your alter ego
Will you marry me? You'll get a huge diamond
And a peony dress sewn with vines

An affiliative gesture
Elephants put the tips
Of their trunks
In each other's mouths
And swirl them about

It's a marriage exam
Dead black-eyed susans
Look good covered with snow
The tango pit's covered with egos
I wish the untouchable skeletons were geraniums

Plant pathology
Love is easier than you think
Possibility vs. probability
A pre-verbal sensation
I didn't know what I could do

But then I had a dream
I saw I knew more than I thought I did
Watershed! Away! Ouch!
The tip of your trunk hurts a little
And tree-trunk borers become whale-bone borers

Olly olly ocean free
Can you name what you desire?
Hell-o sharknado, bi bi old id
I began to love you 30 billion years ago
But what did I know?

(with Jennifer Karmin)

April 27

Another gray Sunday. Trees turn brownish. We'll think of yellow.
     Yellow as a no-trespassing sign
     Yellow as a goldfinch in summer
     Yellow as a daffodil
     Yellow as an Easter vestment
     Yellow as a grackle's heart
     Yellow as a illuminated letter
     Yellow as a snapdragon
     Yellow as the yellow crayola
     Yellow as an egg yolk
     Yellow as an "s"
     Yellow as Saskatoon, Saskatchewan
     Yellow as a dandelion
     Yellow as a coltsfoot
     Yellow as a yellow house
     Yellow as a banana slug
     Yellow as the sly fox
     Yellow as 33 degrees Celsius
Don't eat the Ganges!

     taref fardt molpab baplom gooset tesoog yoraf
     cuskn nksuc gonitu vaina graco widmit smeluc

     Ethics of Sleep II
Tomorrow's another
1440 evening
    Whenever I had no place
to sleep, I could sleep at the home
for black women artists. I had a room
there, I could do whatever I wanted
there. The sheets were very clean.
I was honored when they asked me to
perform. I was planning to do
something with rings.

James Schuyler's Road Show

In the James Schuyler road show, there's no
dearth of interesting people.
                              I was saying
"Our group leader is very weird" when someone
pointed out he was right behind me. It was the
way he grabbed the lapels on the coat on Vito's
dead body that made him murder a woman in a
cult. Anne Waldman and Ed Bowes were there but
they weren't married yet.
                              Followed by a failed sestina about
bush. The end-words are downfall, fallout, bush,
which, writers, fuck. Here's the best stanza:
        (it's based on a poem by Catullus)
        c'mere all of you, my sestina writers
        I'm coming to you from East Nassau which
        Is having Indian summer, it's 60 degrees and Bush
        Is still ostensibly president of the fallout
        from his lies, I wish for his downfall
        Fuck you you fucking fuck
Bill Berkson brought his dildo to sex camp,
You were supposed to have sex without anybody knowing,
What I was worried about were orgasms
But I could come at the drop of a hat
You had to leap up to go to the bathroom
Bill's dildo was like a sock darner or maybe
More likely a darning needle, all underworld
Queens need bees, blonde assassins
                              There's a female
Farley Mowat there
                    Everybody's speaking
Rongorongo
        What is a vanilla mask?
Everybody in the dream's taking a different drug
One is Soprecin
                I found Charles Bernstein's Pen
on which he had written "property of

Charles Bernstein" then we found his dead body but
he wasn't dead, on the bus you could count things
            the former budget of Bushwick
is being returned to Qatar, sped along by horses
on a boat
                    everybody was going to their after-school
activities so I could be alone with this guy
who locked himself in his room, I don't remember
why I wanted to, you can't figure out who all
the people in your dreams are
                                    everybody drinking
coffee had their own pot, I say I'd like a little
coffee in a big cup but I just get sips of other
people's
            Lewis has to listen very patiently
To what Anne is saying
                            I dream I bring back
From the dream some iced sprite from the kiosk
In front of every elevator door in Peggy's
Ancestral building
                        Turns out we're at 88th and DeMott
We pass a sign: Soon there'll be a junk shop here,
I explain that like those liquidation signs, it's
not necessarily true, I buy a knitted shirt that
says: Look Up At The Sky around the collar –
who should it be for?

April 28

Cloudy in the East. Monsanto has a building in the St. Louis botanical gardens named after it.

WHAT ON THIS COAST IS BEGINNING

To shine like a wine bottle in the trash
This is my concern for the day
And something new in the evening
Another beautiful Copernican gown
for which I am grateful lord
There is a time for everything
Like getting high higher highest
Here in beautiful aloneness forest
The surf remembers another form
of revolution. Nothing. But do
you want to remember the note
tacked on the wall? I am lost
Private property is
not a victimless crime

April 29

It will rain for the whole rest of April. Unlike tomatoes I found the Japanese insect stickers.

culems ocarg aniav bhtilg frayo gmypy

teval   valet
    butter   roffad   fordf   farfad
afford   wltteao   two late

Local Politics

Inspired by the American constitution
I hate having all these motorized vehicles
The farmers in Berne and Schoharie, Columbia
In the field, which no one but me thinks
Albany and Rensselaer counties
Is mine. This is the origin of criminal activity
Decided to end the system where the patroons
The field guy can't stop, he's a lunatic
(the 1%) rented their land to the 99% of farmers
zooming around in his bobcat, he
and extracted crops as rent or even money
fans the fires of my wrath: property is robbery
not just a philosophical stance, the Kinderhook
the farmers dressed as Indians in calico
Creek Bank is lost to the enemy and poetry
to scare the rent collectors, tarred and feathered them
is now dependent on field activity
down with the rent was the cry
nobody join the army of the self-avowed prick
advocates of paying rent were called up-renters
would they? The red-winged blackbirds
because the leases were legal contracts
are beginning to do their mating-displaying
auctions of livestock to pay rent were sabotaged
long ago, in other weather, this here field
by feeding the sheep salt and shooting the cows
was occupied by the Mahican Indians for something
so the farmer would get reimbursed; the owners
but it was still a woods, then cleared for hay
of all the land were Stephen Van Renssalaer IV
now made into a white man's manicured lawn
Livingston and others who could afford to be descendants
When we first moved here, the then hayfield
Of wait, there don't seem to have been any women involved
Owned by an unseen guy from Queens and hayed by Jay
They made the calico dresses for the Indians! The men

Then Janis Londraville bought it and put up signs:
Defeated the patrons and their cronies but we still
"no cutting of trees" then Jay stopped haying, we're guessing
rich people, corporations and the Vatican
maybe the field will become a golf course
owning land and you need money to buy it
we can all be caddies, carrying the owners' irons
the account I read was *Tin Horns and Calico*
least we don't have to be shackled by them; the cardinal's
published by the Berne Historical Society
come back and all is mud now, 4/1/2012
by Henry Christman, whose father was a local poet
I don't think it's right the GBF gets to have
You can also find it in Howard Zinn's *People's History*
The great blue heron fly by his "property"
Of the United States in the chapter called
Where is the luna moth's cocoon now?
"the other civil war" widespread against the rich
the GBF is freaking out now because people swam
in 1848 – people believed all men (at least) were
when he wanted to fish, two women from Fawn Ridge Farm
created equal (except for slaves) and one can lord it over another
rode horses in "his" field then and one fell off!

April 30

      Cold
      For
      Now
Windy nasty and raining too
                     Windy
                      Cold
                          Landscaping
                          Canceled
                                    35 degrees
                          Landscaping
                     Cold
                     Windy
Too raining and nasty windy
      Now
      For
      Cold
April 30
      No buds but bumps
                  But no
               Buds

The Lonely Arc of Whispers

Yeegods! Does not exist, eh?
If such a title can exist, Clarice
How come you never came to NYC to hang out with the big girls?
We're all struggling with the same issues, how come
A "god" let your mother be raped and die of syphilis
Thinking your birth'd cure her? As far
As I can figure humans get stuck with mishegoss
No matter how, when, where or why
The center of this picture is your navel
Of that vase of purplish flowers which
If they came from your navel would be surreal(ism)
Paintings've grown to have schools
Let's skip to the relationship between humans
And humans' "creator," let's say there was none
Why do we all be? Why is each of us just one?
Do we become many, or all, later?
Maybe but didn't we begin that way?
And aren't we that way all the time?
Questions exist as a way of saying
There is no opposite to what I'm thinking
Now I've got it all figured out, I'll die
Happy, rich and loved as the woman
Who figured out everything and don't forget
I have a memory of the future, just like a whale
Future, just like a whale

Tsatsawassa House and Its Front Door

Well what's happening?
The Greens just wrote me
An ambiguous note about the autism society
The electricity's on now
And if all goes well I'll finish the Helens of Troy today
But it's hot and I am wanting
But I am warming up in another way
Far be it from me (the typewriter is too and too high)
But there is light, this is where I'll write
The conversation with the door cause I can see it
From here it is open
My name is Bernadette Mayer, sometimes
I am at the head of my class

May 1

The bookstore in Pensacola was flooded from this storm that caused all
the tornadoes in Tupelo, birthplace of Elvis Presley, and here constant
rain but it's not raining yet. It will be warmer though. And though
warmer be will it.

virlde   ginte   ocive   perpaap   sowhad   serds   funti

barbos   dreeeg   leebv   usise   deymar   fridaa   latsl

May 2

That desperado's a pro, conflation of a drug name and a frilly dress.
Tornado's are a dime a dozen this year, unless you're in them. Unless
you're a pirate, piracy is a victimless crime. The one thing Aristotle was
right about was metaphors. C'mere all you similes, don't go too far! And
don't forget to floss! Like Bernadette Mayer, she was an anarchist but
not the bomb-throwing sort. Grackles are Donald Trumps.

chen   coinri   linenf   kebir   olfro   luvyoj   dounba

serds   funti   yecda   liqtu   nineeg   conpue   geg

May 3

We went to see *Kill Your Darlings* at the Albany University. It felt like
Columbia. Today's Dave Brinks' birthday. I'm mad at him because he
never hears a word I say. He just ignores it. And I'm supposed to be on
his side in his divorce. The bluebirds are doing their morning thing –
acting like they live in the nest-box. Today we'll have our first work-
shop of the new bunch. It's gray. It's supposed to thunder somewhere
around here. It didn't but rained inconsequentially. The new workshop
appeared and everybody talked about anarchism. Anna is going to NYU
in the fall. Now it's a gray May 4th. No sign of the GUBFI.

edlirv   vuri   vlatinoyle   ninoo   fiwts   kodect

hnercw   wcrenh   plapy   cnphi   smagti   torese   geoam

May 4

I finished *Anthill*, the only novel by E. O. Wilson.

May 5

The E.O. Wilson character saves Nokobe, the tract of land in Alabama
where the anthills are. He does this by going to law school at Harvard,
then working for the company out to destroy it thru development.
The evangelists try to shoot him but he leads them to an equally crazy
fellow who shoots them instead, Frogman. Working within the sys-
tem could take money, family connections. Emphasize mutual aid. It's
barely 40 degrees.

wornc   edgred   kawnee   eenwak   murst   siaal   ginodi

idonig   idonro   ornodi   tomto   inray   iretw   koiven

May 6

There are so many leaves in New York city, also so many cars, so much
water. I will never go there again. Bill Kushner showed up for our read-
ing – me, Phil and Marie reading *Hibernation Collaboration* – and said
he'd like to do a collaboration! He was wearing shorts. Also saw John
Godfrey, Don Yorty, Keith Gardner, Mitch Highfill and Adam Fitz-
gerald. We read with inspiring Elizabeth Robinson and ate oysters. A
woman named Charity who works for Jonas Meekas kept threatening
to jump out the window or just accidentally fall. She threw her greens
on the floor. Phil nicked his fingers shucking oysters. Saw lilacs! Some
leaves are beginning here. Saw ZAM, Zola, Alyssa and Max. It could be
Maz. Shazam! Or Mazda.

neviok   taroro   rayin   ladvi   vtelev   ivdal   rabno

seyjs   stopla   etarilseyzt   atubo   woryds   sdyro

We Are Only One Person

The I yearns for addition
Lover money dinner power library
Maybe even a metaphor, Angkor Wat
I get that oceanic feeling from
The ocean to which I've returned
I'll never see you again you commenter
On my lackadaisicalness, my millimeter
Of gaiety at the pub, my
Febrile knowledge of giving birth
Why does knowledge have that 'g' in it?
I lost track like a derailed train
I'm below you now, I'm on top of you
I hope I'm not crushing you
Your limbs might need amputation
But you are not me
I never thought I was you
god does too, that would be fluent
It's god we need to get outta here
Not this yearning for completion
Willowy rascal of the giant phallus
Help! Get me outta here!
      Trying to find water
      Deep enough to swim in
      At the children's t.v. workshop
      Somebody puts me in a car-cart
      But I can't get out

To Have No

What could it be?
Friends? Purpose in life? To live
And breathe, I don't know
The sun's out but it's in
The center of the galaxy or swarm
Or pickaxe, I've got more pizzaz than you
Land? Oil? Universe?
I can rise from the dead, can you?
I got up too early, I'm falling asleep
My father told me to have sex to prove
I'm not gay, my mother told me
To eat, eat, eat famous cucumbers
Resting in a box of snow
Selected by movie stars

May 7

It's the eve of Truman's birthday. Sunny. Buds on the trees, even small leaves. Sunny Harry?

fuiny cripe hstigt tgitsh utelot toletul

May 8

Saw a beaver: first I saw its paddle-tail; I thought it was an extinct platypus,
And people would come from everywhere to see the last phalarope of love.

tretu priew rarebb aicepe squte clugh cudint

liyzla zdiyz conth hegirheralg futsf sidya ggoa

May 9

A gloomy warmth. A glimpse of the future? The lawn-field remains unmowed; it's waving in the wind.

virati neklen nelken aztop htoop unflat droopan

napord dhice cawth hlewat tawehl swyhim mihyws

May 10

Ditto. Only it's gloomier and warmer. The grass gets longer – it's harder to mow when it grows so floating. Mowing gives people something to put on their to-do lists. Rain falls. A warm gloom. Saw a snake.

herigh   glaber   braige   higher   hiragh   herigh

algebra   dznoghiga   gerbal   labger   palpy   tagio

May 11

fucking Mother's Day, eve of my birthday, it's the beginning of the cut flower season. Let's buy things. No more frosts.

plir   smoge   dredger   megeo   amoge   ankaw   moned

omcdined   endom   wreck   o   demon   surroc   ruscar   ru   ro

crosu   scorur   snopt   cercau   bulned   paindry

May 12

Marie and us ate oysters and I steak tartare. The holdout maple gets some leaves. The bluebirds are occupying the bluebird box. We took Marie to Ashfield to her writer's retreat. She's looking forward to a vacation from the NYC subway. She forgot her tea.

nitmen   troded   bedgut   odacova   ague   sacany

dorexted   nibmenl   entin   hrus   piemedcapaum

That tree is bulging out
That tree's leaning toward another tree
They're touching!
They're one!
Once the land is cleared
It should be used for something
To have a view? To set off firecrackers?
So Bernadette can see the wildlife on the other side?
So Phil can worry B will kill the lawn-maker?
She knows where he lives
Maybe he has an alarm system ... a vicious rottweiler
That tree's divided into three parts
This piece of ass wants peace
Peace of ass, peace for asses, ass-peace
Peaceassishness, an end to all cars and zooming
Down a highway that's destroyed our neighborhoods
Piece by piece, ass by ass, does the beauty
Of the landscape create peace? William Makepeace Thackeray
Kateri Makepeace Tsatsawassa
I was asking my gym teacher if we could have
Senior swim instead of senior prom
Turns out she dresses as a fish for the prom
She said no
She said her costume isn't waterproof
Lately I've had a slew of days
Where I miss the mark
I burn things, break things, drop things
Maybe that's what a serial killer feels like
I haven't seen the blue heron in two days
Now I see the gubofi* on his mowing machine
It's autumn but it's June
The guy's a demon
I'll bet he drinks too much instant

*GBF – guy who bought the field
Jennifer told me it had to be a word, like radar, or snafu, to be a real
acronym, so I put the appropriate vowels. I'm hoping *gubofi* will enter
the language, as in everybody has her or his *gubofi*.

Creepsville

Millions of paper dollars
Suddenly come from behind a tree
While you're looking
Under a rock for money
To pay for a gift of pillows

What do the dollars look like?
Purple and orange-striped
Like a sunset at love canal
Invisible except for its hands
I'm afraid of this dollar-thing
It might eat me!

I hope I never
Get eaten by money
So that my essence
Would emerge in its shit

Poem for the Benefit of Me

Thank you, all of you,

For helping in raising

Money in the USA where

I grew up, became one

Of the poets but can't

Earn a living, floods

Are never of dollar money

We'd take just the ones

From the tops of waves

To pay bills for what

The earth's arranged

We'd have for free, if

Only enough poets could

Explain how to do it

I'm trying and thanking

You all for helping

Me pass thru the eye

Of capitalism's needle

Note: A benefit was held for me, organized by Steven Hall – dancers, singers and performance poets. I felt like I should go in a coffin, but I didn't go, I wrote this poem and Brenda Coultas read it.

Sway Bar Blues

Oh sway bar
Another incomprehensible
Automobile part, it cost
$200 to fix so Phil
Can get to his job
To pay the sway bar bill

Climate Change = Text Messaging

OK there's a dark cloud
It's raining but the sun is out
Too early for a rainbow
It was cold, now it's hot
Same day as it hails but the sun
Is out, am I guilty? My case
Is dropped, the cop didn't show up
How could he(not)?
And I didn't not do it then, did I?

A New Season

It couldn't be more of a mess
Here in slush and ice-land, global warming
Or something's turned here NYC-ish
When it snows; the finches, on the other
Hand'd rather stay here for winter now
They gather under the feeder and when
They all fly away at once, it's spring
Or something, a new season called WHOOSH

Wilderness

Wildhahaderahanesshahawild
I won't be wild if you won't
We just won't be wildwinter
Of summersomewhere the wild
Wind willows when whoever ventures to the fairgrounds
With the willow wallowers

On this day of
December 12, 2012
What day is it again?
Will I be you soon? As we turn
The year to one new, will you be me?
Who all'll be the cheerleader?
When the skies get to grey they lose
Their fortitude, I'll willow for you
Who wouldn't? I say if you think
Something three times, move to a different place
Even for a woman, it'd cost a small fortune
Best not to think but
What is consciousness?
It's the drone
Of the hummingbird's wings
Bird's wings
Heard by you
It's the humming
Bird seen by you
It's its nest
You happen upon
And eat the tiny eggs

I Am Proactive Ephemeral Epiphytic Residue

I don't mean to get all
Parallel universey on you
But I am at once the spider
The spider web, and
Me observing them

May 13

In Ashfield we went into the wrong house first; it seemed like a house for bluebirds, I'm sorry, for writers on a retreat. There was a big communal table. Ashfield has a lake but the water's still cold. Pearls are found in salt-water and fresh-water oysters. I got many field guides for my birthday and *The Sixth Extinction* by E. Kolbert and some bacon stickers. Now it's clouding over. It looks threatening. Coming's some rain maybe. The weather knows how cold and slow it's been so it's pretending to still be cold.

nocic   cinioc   cinco

oncic   hashiric

May 14

The full moon of May, what should I say? For this here place, I've been told you can securely plant plants now. We had to wait this long. It's so cold you don't wanna get out of bed. The birdfeeder fell over again, rain. I see a little blue sky though. Maybe the birdfeeder feels as useless as the field. The purple finch is red; the goldfinch isn't gold.

bicest   snolammasoln   erwser   codsen   hondre   dietec

gancey   cagwyn   ageyn   gancey   avewi   snirf   whool

May 15

Last night a spectacular rising of the moon in clouds, then fog, fog so thick you couldn't see the moon.

May 16

The bluebirds are swallows. I guess that's why they were acting so bluebird-ish. We have lilacs!

some   moneyman   iweay   plois   exitoo   bonema   ambeano

inveg   faytes   faytes   geali   cloke   rannem   iaonn

Prehistorically in Prehistoric Times

You couldn't plan to get pregnant
Nobody yet knew about sperm
Men thought they were apart
And nobody knew you could plant plants
Plants grew wherever they grew
Where did I see that jack-in-the-pulpit?
People had memory of all the things
Their tribe had ever done
Including in the past they hadn't seen

Waiting for Dave, Megan and Issa

Where am I
It's supposed to be hot and sunny
But it's cool and threatening
Threatening to be changeable
There's a crisis in the banking system
Of Afghanistan, some people think the president
Of Syria is dead and in Japan old people will
Take over the work at the threatened nuclear power
Plants so the jeopardizing of their health
Will matter less, in years I guess, nobody
Has figured out what to do with nuclear waste
In Denmark it's to be buried and so nobody
In future times will unearth it, the whole
Area will be covered with faux thorns
          Now it is overcast
There's an ominous wind blowing
Wait, everything's looking a little brighter
Oh, no, it's darkening

Theory of Everything

Doing nothing
On the blink
Neither here nor there
Do you care?
        Plastic icicle
        Real icicle falls
        Icycle
Does the sun mean that much?
                Theory of nothing
                The road is white
                Alice's house is white
                Snowdrops are white
                The snow's not enough
                To sneeze at
                Property is robbery
                The car's on the blink
                I'd like to be
                Under the sea

Beware of the Killer Dog

Today I'm just like
A person with a device
My mind jumps from place
To place, I'm doing karaoke
I make the screen go up
To another thought, oops
I don't like this one oh
My! Let's scroll down to
A more Hallmark moment I
Have an app for waterfalls
No I'll go to my sex app

Alice's Driveway Is a Tree

I turn on the light and think
The outside gloom will go away
Everything doesn't
Nor does nothing
It's a dark room in a dark world
But right before sunset
We'll see some rays

Along with the courted sun
Goes my astonishment
My love of this same old view
But who cares if I can go
To ancient restaurants in New Orleans

I guess it'll come back
But don't count on it
One two three o'clock
Four o'clock rock

Grey

I see nothing
But the usual locusts and maples
Evergreens, a white house
Nobody's even walking their dogs
It was supposed to snow all day
But now it's hopped over
To another county, 28 degrees
Somebody shoveling looks like a bush
Smoke coming out of Alice's chimney
I guess they've elected a pope
Bill's plowing us out
I don't wish to be a parasite but
Things are livening up for here
Why do I live here?
I traveled around
And wound up in bed at home
Taking a nap, big storm!
Mr. Ots requests the pleasure of my company
To discuss Edgar Allan Poe
And spiritualism in the light
Of the full moon in his garden
If it gets too cold
We'll retreat to a cave

Tsatsawassa Blues

Sky blue, sky blue-pink
Indigo, Persian blue, lapis
Cerulean, cobalt
Alizarin crimson, pitchfork blue
Blue denim, Blue Danube
Blue ridge parkway, powder blue
Midnight blue, black and blue
Nancy Drew's blue roadster, babe the blue ox
Bluefish blueberries Blue Point oysters
Navy blue I'm not so poor
That I don't have a pourer
For my pure olive oil

Rainbows and Mushrooms

The weather man's afraid to say rain
Today's prediction was "dryish"
But it was is and will be
Raining. The mosquitoes've become
Huge and lethal, trees fall down, we need an ark
Waiting for Max, Alyssa and Marie, having started
Way too early, I'm bored and it isn't raining, I miss
The rain, Melissa and Mike are visiting too,
After we eat gnocchi with artichokes, everybody
But Max adjourns to New York City
      Is a sign of autumn, the water's deep and cold
      For August, green corn moon, grain moon
      Now it's wet and cold, where did I go wrong?
      Max photographed barn wood on old route 20
            I write to kill time (Erik Satie)
            Eeny meenie miny moe, are you a towhee?

Here's a New Kind of Sonnet

> To bewilder the ever-present ladybugs
> And turn supermarkets into galaxies

There's a snowdrop coming up 2/16/09
It's good to know there's hope for spring

> Darwin never knew
> How silly sexually we'd be

It's the only flower you might have trouble
Getting to: maybe I'm so old I won't be able
To reach any flowers this year, even daisies
Will be beyond me: "I'm so close to that Queen
Anne's lace but I can't reach it!" There's always
The special Queen Anne's lace hotline for seniors

> Your corkscrew penis won't fit
> My vagina corkscrewing the other way

Cardinal Flowers

When in the course of human events
I summon up remembrance of the walk we took
I see nothing, I don't see, maybe I was blind
Or so enraptured by the sights of the creeks
How many things can you keep in mind
At once? I said I didn't see those creeks
But I did except I can't remember anything
Now I've both lied and lost sunny memory
So recently stored away in a manger
No crib for bed, the little lord pathway
I wonder if I should drink coffee
Now I remember less than nothing, what
Does that mean? I feel so attabled I might
Be the someone else I threatened my sister with
               Being and nothingness

Could You Bring the Wine?

Our power
Our poor pourer
Our impoverishment
Went out the hungry door
All sentient beings see the sun
And/or feel it, it weighs a ton

Poor on odd days, rich on even
But on the days of the month
That are prime numbers, we get
A little bit the way we're not

Today, poor as church mice
We go to the Hannaford's
Spend fifty-eight dollars and seventy-three cents
For a week's worth of food, the eggs
And cigarettes got with a credit card
             Soon we'll be free-vores and
             Dumpster-dive and glean

A – avocet
B – blue jay
C – chickadee, cardinal
D – warbler (dendroica)
E – egret
F – finch
G – rose-breasted grosbeak
H – blue heron
I – ibis, icterid (blackbird)
J – junco
K – kestrel
L – loon
M – merganser
N – nuthatch
O – owl, osprey
P – pelican
Q – quail
R – red-winged blackbird (icterid), robin, roadrunner
S – siskin
T – tanager, turkey
U – underwood typewriter
V – vulture
W – woodpecker (pileated), wren
X – xerxes walnut
Y – yellow finch
Z – ss saf (mourning dove)

You're Boring as a Blue Jay

Day is night is different
From saying night is day
Today is like a night, tonight
Might seem as long as a day, it's
Raining lions and mastodons the creek
Never floods in July or hasn't but
It might be turning over a new leaf

Next day more rain, all night, rain
It's beginning to seem too weird
Pain at the pump's been replaced by rain
Just to distract you like the inside
Of a fallen trumpet flower to a blue jay
              When's it gonna not rain?
          I can't do without food

Sardines

Is a yellow, red, orange, black and green
Word. I got sardines at the dollar store
Where everything except sardines is more
Than a dollar, for sixty cents, as they should be
My father used to take sardine sandwiches to work
Perhaps therefore, I love sardines, when people
Used to talk about the subway, they'd say
We were packed like sardines which sends a message:
Small, cheap, tightly packed, anchovies for the poor
Or you too can be both colorful and inexpensive as
A really snappy, tiny bright blue convertible
In which you can enjoy the good things about
Feeling like a sardine but maybe you'd rather
Be a striped bass or be a manatee with me
Or a grand whale, forgetful of nothing even
The future or, dimwitted as a human, you'll like
Being so big, the ocean's CEO, you'll take home
A giant amount of cash when the ocean goes bust
So you can share it even with the downtrodden
Sardines who get packed in cans in Thailand
And shipped to the family dollar store for Bernadette

Bill Green

Money's green as grass
Neither grows on trees
But I'll trade you blades for cash

I need to get Bill a snow globe
Of the statue of liberty, we've got plenty
Of tree trunks here, ones with leaves

But no manufactured items except
T.v.s, cars, earth movers and chain saws
Sinks, stoves and refrigerators

Bill's got a generator and a snow-blower
I have an electric typewriter
And a huge inflated bee on top of the t.v.
           Everybody has more money than me
           The tulips are planted by the water pump

Powdered Vermont Cheddar and Celtic Sea Salt

Phil and Hector went to the creek
I didn't go cause it's still too icy
I've been burned by my last attempt
Today a fifty-degree day in February
Last night I dreamt Anne gave me a hundred $100 bills
She had some extras. Sun, no, yes, maybe

On their return they walk to the footprints
Still in the snow without apparent difficulty
And, guess what? The sun comes out
But not for long: the snow's shrunk as feebly
As the sun shines. Let's hope tonight's rain
Washes the snow away so I can walk
        The ice got worse, now what?
        Yellow and green pie with chemicals

First Show Hotline

Out the somber window that shows
Hibernating trees, the water pump, the road
Nothing falling from the gray sky yet
The room I'm in's too clean, the fire's failed
I'm doing the french fries on top of the stove
But mail's failed to come, the turkey had no liver
But it may work to write this poem unless
It gets stuck like a car by the creek

The creeks are over the top, be wary
Of them, of getting mail from a bank
And a flyer from the family dollar store
In which everything is more than a dollar
Except sardines, I don't even have a bank
Account but I saw a rainbow in the woods once
              When the sun got low enough to shine
              Under the earth's cloud cap, I thought
              That's not a bad deal on dish detergent

Oh What

Are you called?
What flower would be a serial killer?
A flower isn't a spider or a killer
Say the tigers but the lions say
A flower can be a spider, but never
A killer though it might kill in a just war
And the locust contend no war can be just
Unless gay spiders can fight in it
But all spiders are gay, say the mythological
Daddy-long-legs. I disagree, my name is
Hibiscus, I grew up in a commune in Krakatoa
You can all go to hell I feel, I mean
You can go wherever you want to go but not here
Unless you want to have tea with me
And the wolf spiders who keep to themselves

Eating the Colors of a Lineup of Words

What's wrong:
Phil's in a bad mood
He has a job
The chipmunk's gone
It keeps raining
No typewriter ribbon
No cartridge for copier
No library books
Ear clogged
Obama might be an asshole
He seems militaristic
No guaranteed annual income
Sun?

Eclipse of the Hunger Moon

Out of the eye of thoughtful waking
The open vacuum isn't erected
A random set of tiny lizards
Surpass one another
Opaque kiwi realities
Not upscale jewels
"there I am"
both London and Callimachus
can't erase anything worse
this lack of acorns, empty worlds, gin
drops the cracking of this sleeping absence
unfolding forth the rickety chairs' drop cloth
my aunt reveals her self
an off-key person cackling like you

Lunes by Philip Good

In the mist
I saw a white dog
No kidding around
I really did see one
It was a
White Labrador retriever
There's a group
Sitting in the German parliament
Called the pirates
They advocate for internet piracy
How come U.S.
Has no Pirate Party?
They're all males
With dreads, or scruffy hairdos
I give up
It's hard to be you

Geology Night Sky

The nuclear cooking of free electrons creates spirals
oolitics or pisolitic, it's a stalactitic wheat sheaf
I vanish into the universe like a wave, cosmologically
while you are a crenellated coxcomb, let's be twinned
rolling into a ball of wind & water, made out of time
crystals all have symmetry, stars'd quickly be damaged
if worn as jewelry, Jupiter's magnetism conducive to the heat
unlike a ruby or sapphire, a painted ball, a Saturnian system
a topaz is not a potato but a potato can be like a heart
the night geology sky, bye bye, the night pigeon sky
the pearly silky luster of your opalescent heart glimmers
like a sequel to a night sky, the prequel being splendent
like an opera in a small hall, the pyramids are closed
Desdemona will collide with Cressida or Juliet in 100 million
atomic structures like a bird of geologic light years
superstring theory might be astrology, the plump indigo fruit
of a crystal system, falling hail of telepaths, it's so unlikely
we'd be here, flat lustrous surfaces orthorhombically
or just minerally archetypes, complex or simple in the breezeway
every specimen can be cut by a knife or corundum till
political spirit fuses with shamanic allies, it's all good
all forms are pinacoids like ice cream cones, the ice cream
takes a chance with absence of meaning through goblins
rather oolitic if not massive. If you drop it though
like tomato plants told eons ago to slow down in 2013
it becomes mammillary, even reniform, then hackly or blocky
copernican modernity swelled with Homer & the Basques
but when it refreezes it grows splintery or botryoidal
     Oh the way a mineral fractures
     Can sometimes help identify it
equal areas equal spaces equal times equal rights for women
their beautiful & often elegant crystal form
universal gravitation has a slow cadence when rolling down a hill
regular geometric shape & smooth crystal surfaces
Melville's whale is Elohim to some, dark matter to my twin
easily broken into a powder by cutting or hammering

I'm in love with the great attractor, my dog Hector
sectile: can be cut by a knife into thin shavings
his free-streaming length determining the size of his grave
malleable: can be hammered into thin sheets like gold or copper
from which hector could become another agglomeration &
stretching credulity till the zodiac devours transduction
minerals with a hardness exceeding that of the streak plate
boll weevils eat the vine that annihilates native plants by growing
too fast, luster is modified by transparency
they float into the sky, ammonia is methane, carbon oxygen
may seem softer than they actually are, or as hard as quartz
in the orgone envelope of the world are flying chariots
the hardness of a fingernail, a penny, an emery board
looms until rewoven as all other mammals, I love you, what's my name?

May 18

Niel Rosenthalis is here, from the Sarah Lawrence poetry festival, we wrote this:

The Clandestine Celandine

Celandine, trout lily, yellow violet – can you fly?
The lawn's to be a field again, says Edgar Anarchy Fairgroundsly

Quick lots or not, each blade is kind of hard
Only in the sense of spring, spring on a card

A Hallmark card? Is a blade a blonde? Is a blonde blind?
Is your heart, your very being, in the Poetry State Forest or
                       the fairground?

Your heart is in the fairer one, blonde, mostly, but
Not unlike the card it waits for you in a shell without a nut

Blonde but not blind? How could a card be in a shell?
Well I'd just like to say, does the sun come out
                       intermittently in hell?

The sun does, but it's not much company, except to trace
The shell, which is the card it turns blank, to save face

I think the card's a redhead, a singing redhead without a head
If the sun's dead, the redhead'd be dead but not a grateful
                       dead bread

Fruit size in portion then? Or is the sun a salad stuck in a toss?
Is the head buck-naked when it sings? That sounds like it loves its boss

An albatross got its fingers caught in a splitter in spring
It was banded and doe-clothed, engaged to be married, evening-ing

"Woe is me" but it wasn't. That is the one gold thing caught
in the song that was the thin glint of a ring no one had bought

Wait a second, I got you this ring on purpose at the fairgrounds
It scintillates, you see, like some luminescent cuts of ground rounds

Thank you again. It's not the rose I though it was cut from
Like good data is a ground mound supremely on the run from ...

Cohokia, a city of many native Americans, we don't learn about in
school
A city of mounds, a city of deer herds, a city of steps, stairs, there's
                          No pool

Without a clock tower to watch over it – sad that we think that isn't it
Better to lay around, foreheadlike, dreaming of peace a little bit?

We've been schooled to think
Who cares? But know
                          War, what is it good for?
                          Absolutely nothing!

Nothing that is it rises from absolutely – and in a pink fit
War shocks us but it shouldn't. Let's sleep on it.

He's going to school in St. Louis. We went to a reading of Brenda's
in the breathtaking fields of Portia and Jared in Catskill. Made a
plan with Peter Lamborn Wilson who can't eat a lot of things, to
bring him to Grace's for our next meal there. No potatoes:
                                              the gubofi's
decided to let the lawn go back to being a field.

May 19

Did "they" change the law because of Bruno? So, you don't have to tell
the truth and risk setting the paper on fire. That's a relief. I've been in
the poetry world too long. If nobody likes poets, will they send me to
jail? The church is cold, eh?

May 20

The church is still cold.

May 21

Alan came by and we did the William Blake tarot cards, then we traded
William Blake quotes. We did Phil's tarot too. I got mostly science
cards, Phil painting. I always feel Alan is trying to tell me something
but I never find out what it is. Always there's the sound of chainsaws.

May 22

Elizabeth Kolbert said that homo sapiens may have annihilated all its
competitors in history, including hobbits, leading to the extinctions of
frogs, bats, polar bears, etc. going on now. A human strangled the last
of the auks. Thunder.

May 23

There was a tornado in Duanesburg, one of the colder places here.
                                Went to hear Tatiana
Richardson read at the Pine Arboretum in Slingerlands
People are so faithful except when they're not.
                    No woman is an island
                      She needs peonies
                    Peonies with pink bows
                    To cover her nipples
                    And a big elongated one
                    Shaped like an obelisk
                    Over her tender button
                        If you get there you win
                                The Publishers Weekly sweepstakes

May 24

Time to begin buying furniture whether you like it or not. Be a good
soldier. Blizzard, a huge Percheron horse who lived across the road, just
went to Schoharie in a house trailer which he kicked at until it pulled
away.

I Hate Rye Bread

Well I turned the paper over
Rather than getting another piece
It's Sunday and Jamey won't answer
Just like Michael
I'm depressed
We'll go to the Berry Farm to buy
Tomato plants
And they'll say hello maybe
I'll buy sunflower seeds
There's a nursery around here
Called the Patroon Nursery, shockingly
I see the chipmunk
Everybody thinks
You have to have rye bread
With cream cheese and lox

The Sexual Organs of the IRS

Bimbos in bikinis on horses at Passover
It's spring breakfast, beware of clouds
It's snow that's wafting like a Geiger-Müller
Counter which doesn't waft but registers the degrees
Of blueness

The sea slug carries a disposable penis
It's a use-it-then-lose-it penis
Like the guaranteed annual income
Promised in the past, not discussed in the present

But oh how could a penis be like an income?
A penis isn't an income but an income can be
A penis whereas your income could never be
A vagina though your vagina could be your income
Get it? There is, in nature, no disposable
Vagina because it doesn't stick out, it sticks in
Like a volcano

A supernova for the workers of the world
Reaching a maximum intrinsic luminosity
An astounding astonishment
Be careful or you could light your hair on fire
How precisely can one measure
An object's position and momentum at the same time

I got a supernova for Xmas
It had two sides, it glowed, I shared
It with my sister, it made our vaginas feel good
At first we were shocked like when you see a creek monster
But soon we noticed we had become spaceships
Cruising into jello like a grape or pear piece

I heard purple Jesus took his ancestral fork to the IRS
A sign around his neck, a choir of angels chanting

PROPERTY IS ROBBERY PROPERTY IS ROBBERY

At the risk of harshing my mellow
I'd like to say
My penis is a tree branch
My penis is an electronic cigarette
My penis is a water balloon
My penis is an obelisk
My penis is a pussy willow
My penis is a monument in monument square, troy, ny
My penis is the great wall of china
My penis is an xmas tree
My penis is a taffeta skirt
My penis is tired and can't get up
My penis is hungry, I have to give it some meat
My penis is vegetarian, tofu only please

Important memo issued
In the midst of a no trespass zone:

YOU ARE WELCOME HERE

PLEASE REFRAIN FROM NOT TRESPASSING

(written with Jennifer Karmin)

Report from the Birdfeeder

One finch
One leaf falling down
Another finch
I broke my ulna; I have nothing else to do
Finch
40 degrees, sunny
town weedwacker
spots of sun on carpet   sunspots
sunspots are now slanted certain slant of sunlight
too bad Ted took speed
goldfinch
I hear Bill's voice Bill across the road
If a wolf breaks its ulna, it's done for
A mourning dove
The chipmunk!
A finch
Many mourning doves
m.d.'s at the birdbath
Phil's adding seed (black oil sunflower) to the feeder
If you want to have three feeders: 1 thistle seed, 1 sunflower, 1 cheap-
est mixed
A chickadee
49 degrees outside
finches
51 degrees
no birds at the feeder
patches of sunlight lengthening
Phil's mowing the lawn
Ours is the smallest lawn imaginable
     Mowed with a push-mower
We need a solarium
Every once in a while a leaf falls down
Some unidentified bird flew away
More mourning doves
A blue jay, hopping

May 25

We're to have a Memorial Day grill-fest for Grace, Atticus, Brenda, Lydia, Erica, Michael Ruby, Sam Truitt, Russell and a person dressed as a bed, a chair-person and a night-table person. It used to be Memorial Day was in honor of people who died in wars. Now it's people who just died. I know plenty of those.

May 26

Today's the real Memorial Day, a national holiday. Russell never showed up nor did Grace. We forgot to eat the clafouti. Alan and Jennifer came.

   cao   sin   soanic

   sanico   sonica   anisco   casino

May 27

A grackle goes to the birdbath, trying to be charming.

        vsrent

           ventaraverent

May 28

Cold for now. This must be a parallel universe (consult T. Berrigan). It may feel cold, I don't have a cold. Blustery, dark. I wish I was a sensitive briar. I made lentil soup and cornbread. Welcome back winter. Winter forgot its car keys, phlox, columbines. Cold4May.

The Rent Strike of 1848

Inspired by the American constitution
The farmers in Berne and Schoharie
Columbia and Albany and Rensselaer counties
Decided to end the system where the patroons
(The 1%) rented their land to the 99%
And extracted crops as rent, or even money
The farmers dressed as Indians in calico
To scare the rent-collectors, tarred and feathered
Them. Down with the rent was the cry
Advocates of paying rent were called up-renters
Because the leases were legal contracts
Auctions of livestock to pay rent were sabotaged
By feeding the sheep salt or shooting the cows
So the farmer would get reimbursed; the owners
Of all the land were Stephen Van Rensselaer IV
Livingston and others who could afford to be descendants
Of, wait, there don't seem to've been any women among them
Defeated the patroons and their cronies but we still
Have rich people, corporations and the Vatican
Owning land and you still need $ to buy it
The account I read was *Tin Horns and Calico*
Published by the Berne Historical Society
By Henry Christman, whose father was a local poet

My Love Is Like a Red Indicator

My love is like a red indicator
That's newly sprung in thermoelectric assembly
My love is like an auto-range interface
That's sweetly played in tweezer tip sets
As fair thou art my bonnie bit drivers
So deep in matrix displays am I
And I will love thee still m'dear
When all the toroid cores gang dry
When all the tubings gang dry m'dear
And the banana binding posts melt with the clamshell cases
I will love thee still m'dear
While the dual alpha-numeric displays display

After Robert Burns

Ode to Wolf Spiders

The spider gets bigger
Closer to my desk
They're more brazen than before
Before was yesterday
Philip Corner, Alison Knowles
Dick Higgins, Steve Reich
Spiders don't seem like people
I get up eagerly to spider watch
They've almost gone too far
If the spider fell
It'd be on my desk
It's spinning a web
Now it's curled into a ball
Outside the window, moths
No lunas yet
It's 3:15 a.m.

Now Is the Time

For all good women
To come to the Okapi Fest
There'll be pastries filled
With whipped cream and raspberries
Today the sun's always setting
Isn't every day weird?
e.g. my clothes have blown away
and everywhere I look there's woodpeckers
the sky wears its cap of clouds
to indicate to us the time of year
I want a dark chocolate truffle
To bolster my reading of the book
About grave-robbing and phrenology

The Uses of Leaves

Leaves must be good for something there's so many of them
I don't mean why do they exist, I mean
Once they're here, what can we use them for, if we can't
Eat them or smoke them? The ginko leaves make good
Cut things in vases, I tried to smoke the maple leaves
But I got a sore throat
The morning glory leaves are big enough to carry things in
Or make placemats for a small meal
Dry leaves are good for scrunching in the autumn*
You can walk on petals, newly fallen leaves make a good pathway
Frozen falling leaves are fun to watch
Good for metaphors, to imagine you are made of leaves
Sewn together with vines, rocks as bones
There's a borer in trees that's become a borer in whale bones
Because trees haven't grown there in 30 billion years
The first time I saw fallen leaves in autumn
The tops were pink, the other sides yellow
Then I saw black outlines around each leaf

*as dry leaves that before the wild hurricane fly, when they meet with
an obstacle, mount to the sky

May 29

Guns bad, bear good, or vice versa. In a camp after WWII, Nazi POWs
sat in front of black GIs. The daughter of the American ambassador to
Germany when Hitler was beginning, was "shown" to him as a poten-
tial girlfriend.

bufial   ilbafu   fsiul

LCHLLILPI

Sorry for the delay, I got stuck in a wormhole.

May 30

Something ate the basil plants; sun on the typewriter. Yesterday the
tree guys who work for the power co. came to clear branches away from
the lines. They readily cut down two of our trees and chainsawed them
up for firewood. Bill had told them I had a stroke. Now we have more
sun on the shady plants. Today's the day the Greens put their garbage
out.

walfed   dewfal   flawed

USETOTTHLFLE

May 31

Eve of June: everything that happened before this, happened before
June 2014. June's eve, WWII ended, I got a watch for my First Commu-
nion. May's last day. Bought a hanging plant of purple and red verbena
and a thriftshop red tablecloth influenced by Downton Abbey.

      unewhounge   unhoge   hounge

enhogu R T H T   wundew   unhego

  unwed   gnouhe   gnu hengu   hengo

ughone

     enhoug   emguho   R T H Y

Two from the Golden Bough

On the first day of spring
Chinese New Year
The governor sacrifices
To the divine husbandman
A bull's head on the body of a man

Ox Pinata

A blind man pastes
Different-colored papers
On an ox
If the paper is red
There will be many fires
If white, floods

Blinking Slinky

There are eight
Xmas lights in Alice's windows
But now there's a blinking slinky tree
Like a blond assassin

12 polluted lakes
11 superfund sites
10 spent fuel rods
9 toxic waste dumps
8 two-headed frogs
7 diseased tree stumps
6 indicted politicians
5 ignited water spigots
4 lakes on fire
3 cancer clusters
2 poisoned landfills
1 globe warming
& piles of dead birds

Two More from the Golden Bough

The Hand of Glory

The dried
And pickled hand
Of a man who'd been hanged
Used as a candlestick
Brings success to thieves

        A woman will dig up
        The earth from the footprints
        Of the man she loves
        And put it in a flowerpot
        In which she plants the fadeless marigold

The Flooding

It was the best of times
It was the worst of times
Forget about worst though
We live in Best, NY, right
Next to the Best Berry Farm
In the old church/synagogue
Nearby we swim naked, eat human flesh
And fuck till the cows come home to scare
Our new neighbor who'll think
What did I do to deserve this
Onslaught of insanity? It's anarchy!
Let's be done with democracy's hegemony
And lace our Guinness with insane champagne

Frigidusaphobia

Mrs. Field
Oil fields
Hay fields
Field guide to
Open field poetry
Field of dreams
Corn fields
Academic fields
Competing fields
Alfalfa fields
Fear of fields
Asparagus fields
Green fields
Ice fields

June 1

Not only that, it's Sunday and the local paper didn't arrive. Now it did: it's still Sunday though.

June 2

Russell Day called his book *Day*: can't wait to point out how narcissistic that is.

> Harold, Stanley and Floyd
>
> Plants pause
> In their growing
> Because it's so cold
> It's dispiriting
> Meanwhile I have to say
> These names all the time
> Harold, Stanley and Floyd
> Two animals, one human
> How did I wind up here?

June 3

It getting cloudy already, 9 a.m. It's supposed to rain all day. Foxes begin to eat things. Bill and Phil finally began to plant the garden.

June 4

Yesterday at dusk, there was rain, reluctant to begin, dramatic winds, a minipower outage and a rainbow. Phil's landscaping boss freaked out and may have fired someone, because some holes hadn't been dug. I got up way too early.

       mustet   stomust   stoutum

stumot   utmost M S A B E E T   beats me

June 9

    El em en oh pee
    Queue are es tea
    Yew tree double yes ex why zee
    A bee see did he feel oh gee hi jay kay's
    Pizza let's go to chez mike's, OK?

It's murky. Phil bought a Pixma because a black widow spider is doing memory with 300 photos but the Pixma doesn't seem to have enough pixels it's raining, once I had a pixie haircut the verbena hanging plant isn't getting enough something I say water Phil says sun the lobelia one attracts a hummingbird every day we still can't get the Dutchman's-pipe vine to make a flower there's flowers on the rosa rugosa bush

                        ackrosouteo
crosue
                        ackrosouoet

soon peonies, I need to get a Hawaiian fruit pizza. Beware of the entry-way to it's pouring the old man is snoring, don't opt out.

June 10

Bramble bushes begin to bloom. The eggplants and peppers get eaten in the garden. Plus a goat gets bloodied in a fight with another goat. The peonies start, the fig tree made it. I think it's raining now, it's like a misting tent. Except it's kinda cold.

June 11

Except it's kinda cold.
Orange prose
dawn, you can be awake, you undress, stay in, the cheerful hallways of dawn, many palpable people, even more, they don't seem to know me, bye, I never sang when I was young, long dresses

blemem   rawtie

waiter   emblem   S T T E S R E M E A T R

June 12

     June's full moon
     Dear diary,
          Some say this darkness is a punishment from god.

        trepu   reput   torte tortea

orteat   rotate   nopuce   poncue

          S L S T T E U E

     She asks a question
     She laughs and laughs

June 13

And it is Friday too. It's the day it will rain all day. Not raining yet though.
disown   emago   entomb
  meago   agome   sionwed

June 14

Went to Michael Czarnecki's reading at the Pine Hill Arboretum – there wasn't enough poetry, mostly a story of how beautiful life is if you're him. Slides with too many pixels and many smiling fellow lovers of life. This time the open reading, which is supposed to guarantee an audience, was after. Cynical I felt. Beautiful roses I saw. Phil's going out the porch door with a ladder. Now he's put another ladder on the porch roof. Now there's hammering. He'd painted the windows closed.

tie point breadboard
rocker switch
toggle switch safety cover
power supply
transformer
toroid core
soldering iron
tweezer tip set
needle-nose pliers
gooseneck LED light
toy motor
autorange interface
banana binding posta
clamshell cases
red green white and yellow game
    switches
heatshrink color tubing
dual alpha-numeric displays
rectifier diodes
matrix display

bit driver
heatsink
gear motor
redundant sata
noise filter
smoke absorber
hot air station nozzle
connector pin crimp tool
security bit sit
step motor driver
analog scope
proto board
alligator clip leads
red, blue, green or amber indicators

power entry module

mono ceramic caps
thermoelectric assembly

June 15

Went to see *Cold in July* because it's cold here in June. It's a riveting,
gory movie about a house invasion turned police corruption plot turned
actor's vehicle with Michael Hall, Don Johnson, Sam Shepherd. We
made the Delaware Avenue scene. I heard somebody say "happy father's
day if you're a father." A red squirrel goes up a tree. Visited the Lloyds
in Germantown, turns out you need electric power to use geothermal
heating, what the fuck? So if the power goes off you still have no heat
and can't flush your toilet! It's a conspiracy to make people pay for
something! Or maybe, if you like the earth, you can't like it because
capitalism will come and stop you. What Tesla discovered about the
earth had his rich friends saying well how're you going to get people
to pay for something? At one point we had five telephone companies,
local, long-distance local, long distance far away, to the moon and to
other planets.

June 17

Unregistered voters of color.

June 18

Colorless voters are registered.

June 19

It's the kind of day, here, where the sun's out before it's not. Let's go on tour. I forgot to tell about the great thunderstorm which happened in the middle of the night the other day/night. First thing I saw was the curtain in the bedroom billowing out constantly. I thought maybe Phil was watching the storm which came with a lot of wind. Knocked over everything on the front porch table. Then I got to watch the lighting while I was trying to go to sleep if I had my way I'd have lightning every morning like coffee.

Every morning like coffee I'd have lightning – imagine if you could ingest lightning? I think lightning should happen around 2 p.m. when you need a lift. The warnings for this storm were so constant and meant to be terrifying, the storm seemed like a disappointment, the guys logging nearby got their big heavy truck stuck in the mud and when they drove out next day, there was mud all over the road, so they swept it away. The sound of sweeping in this neighborhood is a little unexpected. I had to see what they were doing. Today Linda, who owns the land being logged was sweeping again. When people can't mow because they mowed yesterday, or cut down trees, they chainsaw. Sweeping's a childhood sound because in Ridgewood, Brooklyn, Queens, NY, that's what people'd do to their stoops before they scrubbed them, no kidding. It's my madeleine.

Meanwhile we sat on the porches as clean as floors, identifying the models and years of passing cars, then we played stoop ball and bloody knuckles and roller-skated and if it was raining, we put unidentified foods in each other's mouths and had to guess them. I lost on Swiss cheese.

God Did This

Blank paper will you fuck
Phil's gone to allay cabin fever
Without the snow like taxonomy without
The complication of evolution, the barnacles
Had little geese in them fully-formed
Before they became red herons turned
Into lions now you see moose in Hoosick
Who's to say? This filter reveals
Nina Simone singing "I've got my liver"
While a whale is sighted in an oceanic field
> None of this is true, true
> Means who cares? I don't believe
> That objective reality is blue
> Then there was the maple syrup heist

Now is the time for all good men to come to the aid
of the zoo xylophone, here's the tongue of the
giraffe, open wide . . . .

June 20

Poached egg, toast, raspberries, for dessert, the summer solstice, almost, the egg poacher for one egg, from Max, the bread Mastroianni's from Schenectady, we call it the bread with big holes in it, organic raspberries from the market. We went to a free concert in Schenectady of a band from Sierra Leone, years ago, and a guy said "we've been rehearsing this for a week: glad to be in Schenectady." They were called The Sierra Leone All-Stars. Once I made a ham and cheese sandwich to take on some journey for Jamey Jones with the Schenectady bread. He was impressed but if you use two pieces of bread, the holes won't be in the same places, so the mayonaise won't ooze out.

In the backyard we have a snake which is a leaf. The leeks in the garden are weedy like Sophie's new dog friend, Weedy. Marie has two cats named Essex and Delancey. When she split up with Steven, he kept Essex. Without Delancey it seems like a snooty kind of name.

June 21

We had a summer squash, they are yellow, we grew it in Bill and Phil's garden, it's the longest day of year, shall we eat? Phil's going to celebrate Molly's birthday, she's ten, I got a rabbit for Zola, she's 10 months. A hot-air balloon ride costs $225.

The valerian flowers smell sweet like lilies. At the point where our little strip of forest meets the Tsatsawassa and Kinderhook creeks, I often see the great blue heron, cormorants, a beaver and once a snake. If Sarah who's afraid of snakes is with me, I see more. Halfway is the sycamore that a guest once said was dead. It isn't but it's leaning. The forest is dark and many of the trees twist at odd angles, leaning towards the sun, then leaning back for a few years. At the place where I put a chair, I pretend it's my living room with a stream running thru it. Once a chipmunk posed at the entrance to a hollow log there I swear. At the bench which doesn't exist anymore, I saw garter snakes hatching but now that place is owned by someone. There's poison ivy everywhere. Alice, the woman across the road, has a sign "Beware of the Dog," a few feet later is a shrine to the B.V.M. She's leaving her vast property to the Catholic Church. Next to her is Bill who's sharing his garden with us this year.

Dear miss immerse, it's a double-entendre!
Your mention of the sillito scimitar type of
Tree should make you eat ice cream, what's
The name of that flower? What does "mine" mean as in
"will you be mine?" I am a turtle in sandals, does
this mean the end of images? Grilled cheeses?
Sundays pretend to be a bridge between days. I've
Had it:
          the chef wore a toque
          On his xylophone-shaped head
          "do you have any maple syrup?"
          it was back under the figs
          "are you jesting?"
          asked his helper
          "not very" she replied
          "this meth is making me dizzy"
          she said, a whirlwind of recipes
          swirling in the brain of the helper
              by the dumpster
              a lilting lion's ghost's
              jodhpurs queried: "vxz?"
              his friend, the zebra answered:
                  just take a vow
                  and pretend I'm your ex